Familial Animals

Paolo Bicchieri

Advance Praise for *Familial Animals*

"The speaker in Paolo Bicchieri's *Familial Animals* remembers a past in which danger forever lurks and takes control of a younger self who is only just learning to love his world. Even in remembering, these dangers are alive and breathing and haunt us like an 'ape falling on the back.' Through image rich pastorals and road poems, we get an honest and intensely vulnerable voice that asks, 'where else can I hate myself so tremendously.' The collection is a journey in forgiveness and understanding the complexities of how to love the healing self and those who hurt us."
—Preeti Vangani, author of *Mother Tongue Apologize*

"There is joy, despair, playfulness, and a beautiful grief in the pages of *Familial Animals* that explores what is inherited and forced upon us as well as what is out of reach, investigates the self as lover and beloved, as victim and as perpetrator, and interrogates that self with our contemporary world as context.
Bicchieri crafts poems which shine a light through the prism of abuse to refract the pain, anger, and questions which follow long through lives. These poems are candid & vulnerable, they 'write an answer out of this wildfire' even though the lines are filled with 'shadows longer than how long it took to write this down' that are 'thoughtful in the way a sunflower opens' and show how to turn power & abuse into metaphor as in 'how you could do anything you wanted / and it placed the universe in your eyes.'
As a survivor, what I admire most about Bicchieri's debut is how it is able to make me feel: naked and grateful, filled with a desire to be more honest, like none of us were born into this world to be alone. What more could you want from a book of poetry?"
—Kevin Dublin, author of *How to Fall in Love in San Diego*

""'The time for that naivety… is through,' writes Paolo Bicchieri. And so, each poem becomes a mirror for seeking brutal truths in this debut collection, *Familial Animals*. Emergent and confessional in all the realest ways, Bicchieri carves memory from the bone of his experiences--as a son, as a brother, as a lover--until there is nothing left to give. This is a book about becoming human, about failing. It's about 'survivors and surviving… interrogating… thriving.' Never once do we, as readers, doubt that this poet is grappling with the cosmos of himself, as he traces the constellations of his pains, joys, regrets, and ambitions – a Washington boy who has lived 'like a bull's gripped horns dipped in the ball lightning.' These poems are a fragile reflection of what it means to be young, alive, and yearning to grow from the soil of our darkest confusions, and our brightest hopes. Pick it up, read it in reverse, sleep with it – no matter, you'll feel the weight of its truth on your dome. "

—Alan Chazaro, author of *This is Not a Frank Ocean Cover Album* & *Piñata Theory*

PAOLO
BICCHIERI

FAMILIAL
ANIMALS

Copyright © 2021 Paolo Bicchieri

All Rights Reserved. This book or any portion thereof may not be reproduced, in whole or in part, in any form (beyond that permitted by Sections 107 and 108 of the U.S Copyright Law and except by reviewers for the public press), without the express written permission of the publisher except for the use of brief quotations in a book review.

Bicchieri, Paolo author

Familial Animals / Paolo Bicchieri

Poems

ISBN: 978-1-7365167-3-7

Library of Congress Control Number: 2021942995

Edited by: Beth Gordon
Book Design: Amanda McLeod
Cover Art: Daniel Lloyd Blunk-Fernández via Unsplash. Used with permission.
Cover Design: Amanda McLeod

PUBLISHER
Animal Heart Press
Thetford Center, Vermont 05075
www.animalheartpress.net

*For survivors and surviving.
For interrogating myself and emerging myself.
For thriving.*

Table of Contents

I	13
at some rodeo	14
when men tell me	15
Canine Estates	16
my mother's son	17
Pastoral	18
Prepping	19
a fairy garden	20
brush fire	22
my brain is	23
Duplex	24
Purge	25
a pen bleeds	26
after the late night	27
Yakima Canyon	29
a shadow dances	31
How it was in the winter of 2017	32
the body in the day	33
Pineapple	34
scarmanzia/kismet	35
II	37
he should be in jail!	38
the roadtrip where you become glass	40
An Opportunity	42
the spiral of time	44
a dead coyote	45

	red over red means captain's dead	46
	Amtrak 09/20	47
	i'm dreaming / the severing from the protean roots	48
	Sean Connery dies	50
III		53
	in the maze	54
	self portraits in the fall	55
	when I shave	57
	the circular	58
	I watch the elephant seals get born	60
	Crescent City 8:45 pm in July	61
	growth & optimism	62
	I never remember things how I want to	63
	the name of the movie	64
	Acknowledgements	68
	About the Author	70

I

at some rodeo

you kissed my neck in front of my grandparents / it wasn't that you couldn't / everyone laughed / it was that five miles away / someone wept when they heard the crack / the bulls and the clowns were raging / a bottle of lightning on its side / while the pipes bickered apart a noise / a clanging furnace cleaved into an ant hill / you sucked on my little boy neck to show you could / and it taught me a lesson / about how you could do anything you wanted / and it placed the universe in your eyes / so when I'd look at you from then on / I'd see the cosmos in your laugh / and you'd see your son / in an overturned barrel / with white and red makeup / running

when men tell me

they're romantics I feel an ashtray gorge in my heart and an ape fall on my back

when they say romance is for nice guys I puke until my fingers rot and until my throat corrodes

as they show me how it was her fault I look at doors and I tongue for ground molars

before my father tells me again the rose on his shoulder is for the drop of blood brought by the thorn I beg the beast to get off my body to

let it all exhaust

Canine Estates

from my backyard playing
in the sprinkler dancing in
the shade

        he watches he
        touches he hopes
        to watch   &
        touch

in my front yard playing in the
idea these children might be
humans

in my dusty rooms playing with
the corded phone calling the
police

        he knows a blue dot
        doesn't mean shit to
        these blue uniforms

in that red Toyota out front
playing through the idea those
children will never be safe

my mother's son

there's a tension in the reef
a pulling between the coral

whirlpooling in the bathtub as pounds of water settle on backs, bent
shoulders rich with the pauldrons of an undesired gift

a surveyor of ocean knocks on the door
feeling that struggle from years away

the clawfoot aberration shakes and
the tidepool inside carouses its denizens toward morning

two hands drum on runed thighs
a quieting above the water line

a painted nautilus rises from the sea
acres of hidden aqueducts falling toward the tub

you don't like the way I look, and I don't like the way you look, so we're
both doing something right.

submerged ships leave the brackish water
momentum too powerful to sink any hero

Pastoral

Laying in a too small bed
we read Frog & Toad
until night fell on
young eyes.

You always locked the doors
(and checked the windows)
until age came over
vigilant hearts.

The rental was a brick dropped
behind a cop's house.
Cloaked in chain link fence
until familial treasure slaughtered the pig.

Nothing beat those ragged buildings.
Those rentals weren't home,
but you two were there,
so the weight never touched me,

until it did.

The fog rolls in when I squint
to remember what the kitchens looked like.
Sirens shake and sneak behind my eyes when I conjure the water-stained
book so until those noises are put to sleep I keep my eyes unlocked,
pirouetting.

I can't remember the way the houses looked

from the inside.

Prepping

where i'm from there's a lake full of gold which is also a pond full of people & my pops my old man has taken to buying gold because it's that or cryptocurrency that will be salvaged in the flood & people drowned in that pond men who never learned to swim striking out like Michael Phelps and sinking amongst bubbles and kelp & there are great open spaces where i'm from with tree lines that stand on toes to respect the expanse of hay & if a flood is coming the lake will overflow & the gold will carouse through these labored fields & the bodies will still be full of water & they will still be unpracticed & they will be littered amongst the wreck like salmon on a slippery deck & i don't know what my dad will think of that

a fairy garden

is what my father and his second wife call the front yard
after they return from their road trip through Nevada

>the twinkling lines of lights hung amongst apple trees joined with
stacked piles of split fire wood certainly do create an unreal
ambiance, dripping with the black slime of tolkein tobacco,
burning man ephemera

and it doesn't ring well with my brother and me,
his too-big leather jacket and my too-oily unclear and uncertain skin,

the way they dance below the newly named front yard
the same place we hid from the cavalcade of confusing characters

>the paint buckets full of butt and ash, where we
stuck our hands in the moon garden looking for
our roots, grinding composted coffee grounds into
our palms, dredging up rusted brass monkeys and
apple seeds, spit out by cross country boys

magic of madness couldn't last / sometimes it's just one dance / the
rhythm discontented

and it barely rings well with my brother and me,
his wheelbarrow hands scratching his receding hairline and my
barren palms
burying below yellow yarrow to try and find those roots, those seeds,
those anythings
that might guard my father from his grievances, from his court orders,
from his allegiances

they don't party beneath those shining baubles any more

the music long faded and the fairies gone back to whatever
castles they crept from

i'm not sure that in their escape there was ever any place for roots, for coffee grounds, for seeds to split into sycamore

brush fire

a dozen acres of burning weeds are
like a gray platoon of ash

with no Wednesday and with no allegiance to
anything bigger than a glass of wine

I'm eight-years-old or howeverold I was and
you three were just older, bigger

some damn thing had to give and
it's okay it was me

watching from the deck I thought "I'm
too weak to help"

and watching from the deck tio said "It's
true, whatever you're thinking"

the fire burned Badger Pocket from tremendous
to mending & I cried

however old I am now I'm still crying with no allegiance to
anything bigger than a glass of wine

my brain is

a pipe bomb. Unassuming. Chittering then silent. Present of ticks before an explosion. Homemade. Irish, a murky collection of ancestral pain beaming optimism loud and huge in the decade of today. A gamble. Maker's hands knew violence. Blinks in red numbers. Patchwork effort against a rainy, vibrant homeland. Re-wireable. Symbolic like the hieroglyphs in Cholula that prayed to Tlaloc that came out of the earth with those children and those children maybe they're the ones that drew those symbols and maybe they're the ones that gave my abuelito his brain so maybe they're the ones who, with Tlaloc's divine palm, pushed the Irish in my head into this sunshining riot. The dark rooms that fashioned it are full of light and cannot be filled with ink again.

Duplex

borrowed wheelbarrow of wet
concrete poured around watermelon
gardens planted by second wives
upon return from Mazatlan

this is not a duplex or maybe it is but it'd be happenstance,
a rare circumstance of an unmentioned thing meeting an unresearched
thing to make some
unfinished thing

my face laying in portrait mode and my father's second wife still returning,
still returning, and when she offers us both $100 i tell my brother you just
made $200, bro, good for you, bro, and the word slips into miasma, the
gilded age's germ theory a cloud of unspent money, a jarred sentiment
meeting a foreign mountaineer who

borrows the neighbor's wheelbarrow

needs it for a job. kneads water & rock
to make risers for a plot of land.
stokes seeds into earth.

           once she gets back from
           Mexico, but at this rate
           I'll never stop replaying
           the first part, so dubious

Purge

masked in vomit and ribs
thrown apart gin and wine
Fast Breaks, Ben & Jerry's, peanut butter quesadillas,
smeared in brown sugar & honey.

each day I'll pay
with a walk through the desert.
notes kept in Gideon's Bible:
black ink

If you once loved me:

        The past dries like
        unsunned cactus arms, thrown in needles
        until we look over our shoulder
        and it summons to life,
        robust and desert-gorged,
        Bulls in August
        Jazz in July.

sorry if you hate me

    and if I hurt you.

sometimes I hate me,

        and know that I have hurt me, as you were the one who
        watched the dime of my youth spin on the all-night diner
        table.

(excess: obsess;
the need to loop.
Scribble the fire out,
the red beetle of ember a thing of smoke.)

a pen bleeds

blue & black / a knuckle sandwich of squid ink / a chorus of signatures / a thousand days of diaries / but when will a pen make life vibrate again? / my therapist has me write intentions each morning / reflections each night / prayers in tracings of Bic & Paper Mate / and hey I got off Facebook when I went to treatment / and hey I couldn't handle those looping of blue & white in that logo / and hey that was back in 2014 before shit got analytic / and I ate all the lunches they made me make for me / all the curves returning to my body as the origami of my disease unfolded into my nonna's calligraphy / and I wrote recipes in red pen to catch my attention away from my swelling stomach / and with every pen I've written with since I've ventured

>"I love you" and
>"everything'll be okay, king"

/ but I'd like to write an answer out of this wildfire /

>"when does it stop?
>the stalking?"

after the late night

Lo siento, let me
try again.
                          My father and brother
                          sleep in the other room the
                          lap of the Pacific still the
                          gong in the palace.

The shit smell of the toilet releases serotonin
in the wildest of ways– where else can I hate
myself so tremendously?

Knock knock

"You okay?"

"I'm great."
                          The reaver doesn't believe me nor should
                          he – I rest for a moment with three fingers
                          down my throat volunteering as tribute.
Knock knock

Scars in the fields between my fingers
burnt flesh on cookie pans warm smell
of ginger snap lathered in Pillsbury
frosting making gluten-free moon pies
to marathon Bojack Horseman in
one sitting

Knock knock

"I wish I were dead"
I tell my friends after I finish gorging.

Knock knock

"I'm coming in."

"No, I'm okay."

Knock knock
                    Cotton candy blueberry ice cream
                    a quart of freezer burn worked on
                    by padre y yo at abuela's
                    some Christian Bale movie streams as dad
                    snores

"This is the last time," I promise out loud in
2015, head slicked in the sugar skull bathroom.

I'm sweating and crying in the Nacho Borracho bathroom in
2018, irony adrift.

That anyone stayed around as long as they did
bewilders me– the split bus
schedule of my brain asking to go
away, to go to sleep.

                        but it's not pitiable, these
                        erratic exhaustions

Yakima Canyon

The cattle in the canyon stank of death

let me try again
      very very sorry

The cattle I drove through the canyon stank
a snake spit in my face, coiled
cordless phone beeped ahead of
the cliff face and proud boys cast

flys in the river like they were Jesus
like letting the waters course around
gum boots was holier than walking on

let me try again
      very very sorry
let me drown it out

let me
      very sorry
      very very sorry
      let me
      drown
      let me drown it
      let me try again
      very
            very sorry

canyon slick in ash, a notion of blackness

      numbing it, the water
      numbing it in a viper bite
      a vibration

very very sorry / let me try again

I drove the cattle and there were
water walkers wading / waiting
let me go / let me drown it

try again, very sorry

a shadow dances

but it's just a snowflake / but I have to pull over / and you have to drive because I'm not feeling myself today / (and I don't mean to say I'm not "feeling myself" today) / I mean to say there's a blight forming in the back of a skull I used to own / but I can't extract it / I can't remove the sick / so if you could drive I'd be grateful / so I can sit shotgun / and I'll think about a shotgun / and you'll tell me how to use it and I'll think about nights I can't picture and we'll look at statues built by Italians and by Mexicans that / nowhere near this mountain pass / cast shadows longer than how long it took to write this down / and we'll sit and wait to see if any of the shadows dance.

How it was in the winter of 2017

Pick cacao and throw
ten tons of elephant maw
in the same bucket.

I'll tell you when the rain
falling on tormented cities
stops.

Pray for it
but don't expect it
the time for that naivety, gin and simple syrup on the porch,
is through.

Sell plasma and draw blood and
watch tickets burst into rent checks

and broken cars and yell
yell the whole time.

Yell. yell. yell.
Call me the unborn on Dearborn.

the body in the day

I've got Jack Nicholson hair and 1 want to be honest and say I've got acne scars like cup holders on my temples like I put all that liquor on my fingers and tried to focus and I want to be honest and let you know my penis curves like an unfinished inflated balloon animal and there's a face on it with two winking eyes and let me be honest when I say as a kid that was hilarious so I'll tell you once that on the days I am ready to lay down and be done with myself I remember how each day is one more than I shoulda got and this set of ragged parts has kept me shuffling for 24 and hey let me be honest I'd love 24 more

Pineapple

what a man
                        tilt your papaya head
                        & scream your pride.

Mexico City, too.
                        Goodbye over & over again, honeysuckle tropics.

a gin-soaked protest who
trades coats for cactus on the
sharp edge of a moment.

Pelican swoop, too.

                        Thought about the bear
                        nestled in the sand dunes,
                        the couple's walks on
                        train tracks in Thorp,
                        Washington.

I write the saddest lines between
lush tomato & zucchini between
She & Her, He & They, between
Hercules & La Croix Boy

                        and this is the world for a while.

scarmanzia/kismet

I have decided there is a power in forgetting

that the yellow painted leaves of Central Oregon at 6
pm have more to teach than reviewing the notes

of the last twenty-five years of my life like antique
photos of the Salish Sea

I have decided a happy afternoon with my love
who is thoughtful in the way a sunflower opens

      only while the sun visits

is the revolution of a sick mind thickened in the
granular granite tunnels under the Cascades

I have decided ease is liberation and
I'd like to be a freedom fighter

II

he should be in jail!

in a step toward regularity
you splash forward in aberration

i languish in green hills,
stripping the tannins from persimmon into cinnamon,
mashing the impossibility into marmalade

biking through cold warm streets
packed with absence, you let me
bathe in the memory of your arms,
the melted tip of tamarind paleta my abuela
made me chase down, block after boiled block

i ease my hips, my big thighs, these
womanly lovely shapes, into the fizzy
salt of your hands, a
spa of your wet

i don't know what it is i call fire any more
but i know i love your heat

once i'm enveloped in the ray of your sun,
the turquoise of your fingers gripping my skin,
the plush of my back oozing between your tips

i don't know why they care
that i don't know
and that i don't care

all of that jarred and held
in the trembling voice of my people's cries,
the landless songs

while i'm in a seat of regular light,
you splay yourself in the bedroom,

dripping

the roadtrip where you become glass

so i'm eating a breakfast of black beans and tortillas when the world stops turning

when the street cracks open
when the wind stills and blackberries burst

the sun is sheer like xacto and work starts in thirty minutes, i remind Pops

"why does my family hate me?" he asks anyways

i drink the Twin Peaks black coffee
and the postcards sit unsent south
in Big Sur when shits gets real

when the punctured armor looses the heart's cauldroned tar
when the island rots and the moon eats the garden in the front yard

the city doesn't mind that you assaulted that man, i tell Jose, the bones are done aching in fact they're underground now deeper than a whale resting on a loamy bed of salty earth, i tell Joseph

"you've always judged me. so does your brother. the only person who ever loved me was Amy," he spits. it's three in the morning and he's been on a bender, shaming me for not doing as much MDMA as him at the Oasis, the go-to club South of Market. shaming me for not being a more accepting son. i really wish his second wife's name wasn't Amy, that shit hits like Denise or Cindy, but i don't have the breath to laugh. i'm crying with the remaining shaky breath in my sandpaper lungs.

so there i am slapping the plate with the last shred of the last tortilla

when the white knuckles go brown again
when even the brown can't keep stable and shimmies into bourbon
we both get in that zombie van and
the road hits me like a stack of maple-syrup-wet pancakes and

i fall back into the dream of breakfast, of the day i might have if things veer different this time as i
devastate through the 101.

An Opportunity

the last time I waked and baked,
or is it woke and boke?

it was the last time i did wake and bake
and i was wandering around the lowland desert of Washington state
a place most people do not know
has a desert in the fry-oil smell of a music festival

a man approached me with an elder wand of a blunt and told me

"opportunity be knockin'"

i did not know this was a lyric from Action Bronson's hit single
and I would not know this for two or three years

so for the following two or three years i lived my life
with an impatience, an insistence, an impossibility
i would frame it through the crystal of

"opportunity knocking"

and i lived like a bull's gripped horns dipped in the ball lightning
that killed my abuela's uncle
and i managed my life like a fox,
ripping heads off chickens
and i rolled around the streets like a nighttime friar
finding speakeasies in trash cans

but i don't live like that anymore

       i play banana grams

i "take it easy" when older men tell me to take it easy

i quit buying and selling the little bags with skull and crossbones painted
on them
        and a sidebar for the men who sold me those bags
        wasn't that a little on the nose? the images of the dead?
                we were already on the nose, weren't we?

i don't drink all night anymore

actually i do
i still do that

a 90-pound woman brought minibar Svedkas this   big   to my house
and we danced through them and through Golden State Ciders and
flashed through the Lyft and crashed through mai tais at Li Po and we
blazed through the dance halls on Polk and we sundowned in the Sunset
and smashed the cans in each other's faces in the street light like it was
more than just drinking like i was more than a denim-jacket wearing busy
body masked in that Portland-ass whitetooth covered veneer son of a
bitch but I'll *never* be a son of a bitch because i was raised by Trina Marie
Lanegan and that's a name you remember because on her heart is tattooed
the words "it's a God thing" and on the other side of the coronary it's
written "that's my fucking son" and she stitched those messages onto
anyone who looked at me funny

and when i looked at her funny she stitched them onto me
so when i see opportunity knocking i just call my mom

and i don't go to music festivals anymore because i'm told Coachella sucks
anyways
and i might drink all night after a day of taking it easy but in the morning
i just call my fucking mom

the spiral of time

is a cyclical portraiture.

for example,
>you wish you could remember what color my eyes are.

>but you know my eyes squint in the same way my mouth crescents into pink when I've drunk too much gin. you know they split an atom whenever they respond to the call of your yawn. it's known my eyes vanish like moral support when my mom tells her church she's keeping the baby. my eyes went horizon-wide the first time they were sun-bit in my nonno's front yard, a croquet mallet rising from my chubby grip. when the first, third, tenth therapist played out that sitcom cliche of puppets patting each other's crotches my eyes thin drawbridges drained a few splashy streams. when Pops rears his head back, laughing to exhume ten tubs of loose leaf tobacco, three bottles of Bulleit, one tab of that *good* shit, man, his eyes that are the antecedents of mine spread like the i in thin toppled over.

>and my eyes are dashed in finger-tip hot sauce and back-of-the-hand rubbing that break through the thinness of the weekends spent making sense of the doom, making sense of the strange same in the new. the creak of my rusty eyelids still slicks with gin, only difference is in the date on my phone when I summon Lyfts at 1:46 in the morning. the yawns I pick up in my face echo from yours, not *yours* anymore, that yawn sitting on Yesler Way with that asshole Macedonian landlord.

>and I knock myself into tomorrows with croquet mallets that I swear to god are the same ones I squinted against when I was six-years-old.

my eyes hold some color, but below the snow blind of repetition, maybe it's not the color of a painting that matters.

a dead coyote

lays in gold frost shimmer
outside the sliding glass door

this is not an elegant transition
so I wonder at the way life evaporates
from a muzzle laying cold dead
like the briefness of a handshake

this is not an elegant transition
but I remember my Nonno like
bloat fur were the spindle of beard
lolling from his cancerous nose to his
crucifix chest

this is not an elegant transition
the way we are brought from
powdering birth to fluorescent stillness
frigid and sterile truncations of paradise

so in the pre-dawn dew when I see
coyotes in Golden Gate Park, rolling
the skunk off in grass I feel a warmth in the cold

like hot blood slipping
beneath matted hair invites
the air to return to the puncture

red over red means captain's dead

red over red means captain's dead
it's from the codex / sage burned through chuckle
trawling of a drowned behemoth

we stuffed cigarettes in our belly buttons
the ocean fat / the beaches drunk
red over red means captain's dead

we practiced karaoke like cats carrying birds
a ninth life spent waving adios, mother fucker
trawling of a drowned behemoth

bodies drawn of salmon net
pork buns fries in oil gargled by chicken feet
red over red means captain's dead

night concrete on Ali'i Drive
far from the cocoon of humid coast
trawling of a drowned behemoth

Atlantis is nothing to the sea mariner
who gasped for oxygen below the ozone
red over red means captain's dead
trawling of a drowned behemoth

Amtrak 09/20

with enough time to take the self and tuck it to bed I realized my dad was drowning in a desert & my mom was the most talented woman who ever lived or at least who came out of the Tri-Cities and at least I know the Tri-Cities aren't really cities & at least you learned that today &

with enough time to see a beetle on its back with tiki torch legs playing an invisible piano I realized the lifespan of said instrumentalist is 30 days & my nonno put in 91 years so what's that about or at least I know what an elegant death looks like & at least you can find out too &

with enough time to understand some shit Google can tell me with seven different keys that can't unlock any doors I realized water runs off marble in the same way Ganesh throws worry off his pachydermic face

i'm dreaming / the severing from the protean roots

it's always roots
images of plants
language of lilies

laying horizontal like a coast line
smoking my mouth into bitterness
eat the nasturtium / coconut curry tang

i'm dreaming! life a paced cage
year spent imagining cedars as
totems of coming home / Inception
is just a movie, but the waking up
reminds me of lying in headboard bed

> in dad's converted garage
> my bed was a slab of pin stripe foam
> at the foot of big brother's bed, where we
> assimilated with dad Domingo y Lunes nights

i'm dreaming. the connection to plants is carved from cedar
yet i'm pining / bad joke / plywood pretending to be Washington conifer
but i really do miss it, the burning of split timber in ash wet circles.

bocce with Uncle Ruben in the backwoods of British Columbia
a moment in the garden / i wonder if the ark was built of willow

man i still think i have all the answers
man i still just want to make my cousin's belly laugh
and *man* i loved those days of driving through Ohio smoking weed in the
Pontiac Vibe on the way to Ianni's wedding

and we played North Carolina's own Root Ball in Raleigh that summer
and i'll never know whose roots the game referred to, whose pretending
we explored

and i'm not sure i'd want to know what those earthy placements meant to
the bartender

i'm dreaming / wishing my roots were of kelp rather than birch

it's always plant bound
but a backstroke can be useful
jumping off an Irish coast with my brother

i lay in a gravel yard and wonder if i'm suffocating
not waving but drowning / a poem placed perpendicular
running into concrete walls like birds of paradise in Baltimore

pine trees are just trees, but the inhalation of syruping sap
stakes crystal in the nose just the same. church a notion
not a place. sheep jumping through the Hobbit rivulets
as i carpenter a
cathedral of
chamomile

Sean Connery dies

and no one wants a poem about him.
It's 2020 and we've learned the ways
    one year can betray
    and sink

a thousand times over, like how I thought
2016 could get no sicker when the dishwasher
rot gave my mom chemical pneumonia
•
it's like watching Mad Men drenched / in Freudian formaldehyde / the Scot strut / nationalist NIMBYism / cigarette strike / backhand / martini romance / Crab Key off the Jamaican coast / nuclear armament / i'm shaken
•
ending a life spent in famous infamy
alone in a year infected must be like
rallying the boys for a final hurrah
at a landscaping company
rather than a palatial
hotel, makeup
running, hair
dyeing
•
a woman beater dies and I hope with him goes the misogyny in me / the kid who put $9.99 James Bond DVDs in the shopping cart / Pops letting me push the basket / feeling free & manly as I sailed across the pavement in 2001
•
My ticket to Scotland was cancelled this year
for aforementioned reasons.

We AirBnBd a cottage on Islay
epicenter of scotch

and I'm drunk enough

to give it an undue symbolism

•

when I hold a cigarette in my mouth
does my lover fear me, too?

III

in the maze

there's a volcano with fertile earth.
magma struck sun rocks become

rich soil making the gold coast
amazing, crossing, looping for
the men in pursuit of bourbon and gesha,
arabica, canephora.

there's a solstice in your hands
hooves churning ground like fertilizer
the minotaur in amazement of maize, mint,

indigo, tobacco.

stalk the foothills of the mountain,
search for lace & thread, trace of lead
gunpowder, flint skipping ahead like
baked bread coated in rum jam on window sills
on porches on plantations on doughy pastures
rising with the swell of wild yeasts.

in the maze the minotaur is in amazed gaze, lazy laser
eyes praise the penny pinches, the picket line inched, the

yard boy lynched.

there's a solstice in your hands
palms cupped extinguishing light
like pot top on boiling water,

molten earth tremor down the slopes,
the violent pressure the land below a milled eden,

parchment papering the wind.

self portraits in the fall

as an homage to my inspo: for how long do i look to my curly haired beach-bitten friend to shine light upon me in orange plastic chairs outside the Venezuelan cafe on Hugo?

as a Tolkein-ass pipe smoker in the yard: slats of sun fuzz my eyes through American Spirit smoke because I am *indeed* that kind of asshole

as a cat dad: i hate the way i grab the baby by the neck and bark no / i hate the way the re-direction works just as poorly as when i re-direct myself

as an amateur botanist: i've spent two years looking at the same red fruit-bearing tree wondering what type of mammoth it is
i've spent two years looking at that tree wondering why i can't shoulder my ego into Googling the enormous spire

as a cat dad: how can a white man possibly father a child if he reads the news? if "parenting" a kitten feels like shirking joyful bounding into exasperation?

as a bicycle: stretched muscles wrapping my hands is the only way i feel useful anymore

as a blue heron: everywhere i go feels like home which is the way i know i'll never know place

as a piñata: we swung at roped paper every Easter with la familia and it was never enough to coax abuela out of Wisconsin

as a cat dad: he sleeps like a cotton ball of fog and i pray for peace

as a White man: i pace in the yard and smoke American Spirits and follow the guilt / follow the shame / fever it into tithing / excavate embarrassment like fracked tar as a white man: think through the intonation / think through the raised hand in Zoom / think through the clinking of coins / silver / think through the way my partner is committed to ending the patriarchy that made my nonno's eyes shine with glee

as a white man: telling my partner my celebrity crush is Sza / loving her galore / the other white guy at the party says she has beautiful hair / watching her music videos / sit with silence

as a white man: the diaspora is wide enough to hold my father's assimilation the way abuela reminded us Cortez is our forefather / the way blood inks the present

as a cat dad: clean the empty house again as mio ragazzo trots at my heels, my wizard familiar

as a stairwell: i feel as empty as the tunnels below Seattle
a city built upon hollowness

when I shave

I dance through my bones
and know freedom really *is* free

the bathroom rents by the hour
while the Lyft costs $500

but the liberation of release
is as priceless as Two Buck Chuck

cannoned through my blood
and the corner store light make me king

of breath & water
of Marvin Gaye & John Denver

like the shimmy I composed
in the sixth grade locker room

made me less gay
and more prophetic
                of princeliness

the autumn mist
burying my beard into

ballet & prayer

the circular

there are circles to this puzzle:

If Mexican coffee growers plant coffee at 900 meters above sea level,
where will they go when the acid washed seas slack away their copper
hills?

They may go to the cloud forests on high,
some Mononoke dreamscape, but as the
11th largest producers in the world,
what would Diego and Frida think?

They may meet Homero in heaven
and ask him that same question Biggie Smalls did ask:

> who shot ya? He might look to Nagi Daifullah
> who could lock a broken finger at a colorless cop
> who, possibly, would say that the beans are seeds,
>
> and robusta was just what colonists called canephora to
> make more money out of Virunga's butterfly-infested
> home.

If the butterflies joined these angels in heaven,
amongst bruised hands & straw sacks, they
might descend from those cloud forests
to their coppery hill homes in the
forms of rain.

They might be encased in a slickish sludge and
that rain might join the sea and
it might brush its oceanic
brush along the coast
line and eat away
their terrestrial
home.

so there are circles to this puzzle:

what might happen if the campesino might might burst into reds and yellows and those colors *did* run, ran into rivers of colorful molasses which flooded the melting ocean line into a sweet broiling anthem of

never again &
never forget?

I watch the elephant seals get born

It was in January and I watched 2019 blink into past

lubricated blue crescents writhing around the sand

castle down 101 holding court high above and afield
tennis,
        untouchable & opulent, lifestyle

I wondered at the way my love teetered from heel to toe at seeing the
calves mewl, at watching them hunger

I wondered at the way my love for my love teethes along her arms,
between her tattoos, between the places I knock and wait

in the bombing slams of their father's bull bellies I wondered
about the food eaten in the long halls of Hearst castle down the road

the tide rises each year and I watch the sand,

      dollars,

               grate against the fortress door, futures in oil and in
               children trading below a pint of beer, Brent bent low like
               fentanyl, the opioid that crushes the hillside, the valley, the
               North Seattles all but the shimmering castle peak, mirage

I watched the elephant seals get born and I wondered if any of this
mattered

and I wish I meant the writing or the watching
and not the writhing,

      the sand

Crescent City 8:45 pm in July

I drink green sauce out of the back
of a cracked taco shell and your
dad's Volvo leaks nostalgia out
of the sunroof which is too bad
because it is too new and the coast
etches on like a painting

and what of honey? cracking out
of throats from highway crossed
bears smudging the barrows?

and I want to talk about the smoke
that makes the bees syrup their
honey into hexagons. the funneling
of smog. pipe. baptism of fume.

and that inked pressure slathers
the streets of Oakland, Brooklyn,
Seattle, CHOPing the blocks into
barricades, boroughs into beehives,
milking pain into laminate,

loving a summer with you
while the streets shatter.

growth & optimism

hydroxychloroquine is brought
to the untouched tribes of Brazil

the Javari Valley is kept
away & above the torpedo of
globalization

until now. The populist pugilist
decides the remedy, the chronic,
needs to be given to the unclothed tribes

yet in the Ache of Paraguay children die
on the forest floor, below the rubber tree.
and yet in the bays of Alaska the Lummi
people drink bottles of Jack Daniels until
their blood runs honeyed amber. and yet
in the bay of bays, San Francisco, the syrupy
intelligentsia cannot do more for the Ohlone
than mention, before infrequent city supervisor
meetings begin, with a laugh and a rib, that, yes, the
text books lied, we are still on occupied
land.

so let us pray / friends / take heart / grab hands / clasp tight like giant
clam on sea floor / below the oil fracking sky / that the evangelist,
brutalist, optimist in each missionary & visionary who brings the cure /
the chronic / to the untouched tribes of the forest / that they may also
bring an apology / wrapped in red silk / covered in ten tons of gold &
maybes

I never remember things how I want to

so it's now that we've stopped quarantining together that I find a forgetful attention-seeking boy in my fluttering arms / in my soldered nails / in the way I need you to tell me what they spoke

for I know you won't remember either / the blemish of our divided neurodivergences / the budding / the blessing

or you might remember • remember the way you found me • me, soaked in Jameson, looking to get licked by anyone who pressed against me long enough • enough of me to go around from Castro to Sunset • sunset makes me think of you • you letting me borrow Insert Boy • boy in my hands pushing against my backyard sunburnt white & pink looking for the Houston brown of yours • yours enough to keep me whole • whole years spent in your eyes

the name of the movie

yo Uncle Carlo wants to have a fire
call the dogs, and the neighbor's dogs, and put on Bill Withers
call my dad, he loves this shit
the bullshitting, the laughing, the celebration

but throw out that old bourbon, I don't want it near us anymore.
I don't want to talk about the buried sadnesses, but let's
drink yesterday's treasures, and I don't want to tell stories about
"romance," but let's sing of lovely days, and I don't know
where the night will lead, but let's mapmaker our ways through the misty
night.

here's one – Nonno sailed with George Bernard Shaw. This is a dude who
cradled his thumb over a hornet on the sunroom table to crunch stinging
life into memory and I think about that whenever I need to do some
hardcore shit.

another one – Pops sailed with a generational gout clumped on his knee.
not to call out a buried sadness, just to say the guy kept his eyes to the
stars and in the constellations he battered gas giants into cakes and he
prayed to orca whales with their celestial bodies and that's a story or
whenever I need to remember how to go, not where.

and another for you, primo – you sailed with the salt shocked hair of a
Spanish forefather before your father ever did and when he joined you on
those watery Pacific bastions he wretched and knelt and you sailed him to
shore and I think of that whenever I go to older men for guidance because
even fathers throw up their hands in deep water.

but, you all, pour me another red and let me tell you my girlfriend is a
thinking star, I keep my eyes on her as I charter the dark, and, all of you,
sometimes I can't tell if she's Whitney Houston or Kendall Jenner, and,
my family, let me tell you I pray for the determination to be a harbor for
her as she is a light house for me, with lips like grapefruit sugar scrub.

not to call out a romance, but on top of all that went before, at the summit, there is love. and, all of you all, there is a place for us above the marauding of cacophony and deluge.

the fire's on? Pops, get out here, man. I'm a little drunk on this wine, man, but I gotta ask you:

what's the name of the movie where everything worked out in the end?

Acknowledgements

Grateful acknowledgement is made to the editors of the following publications, where some these poems first appeared:

Harpy Hybrid Review, The Headlight Review, Forum Literary, The Racket, Feral: A Journal of Poetry and Art, Moon Publishing, The Honey Mag, Ghost City Press, Quiet Lightning

Thank you to everyone at 826 Valencia for the work they're doing, to my partner for being the healing light that is her namesake, and to my family for being the beginning and the ultimate.

About the Author

Paolo Bicchieri is a white latinx writer living on the coast. His writing has appeared in *Eater SF, SF Weekly, Standart Magazine, Ghost City Press, Quiet Lightning, Bay Area Generations*, and more. He is the co-founder of the reading series Something Ordinary. He is the recipient of the 2019 Bindle Award from Nomadic Press and the Teach! Write! Play! Writing Fellowship from the Martha's Vineyard Institute of Creative Writing. He has spent time organizing with campesinos for Communidad de Communidad and recruiting volunteers for 826 Valencia. Paolo is the author of three books of speculative fiction. This is his first book of poetry.

www.ingramcontent.com/pod-product-compliance
Lightning Source LLC
Chambersburg PA
CBHW060217050426
42446CB00013B/3097